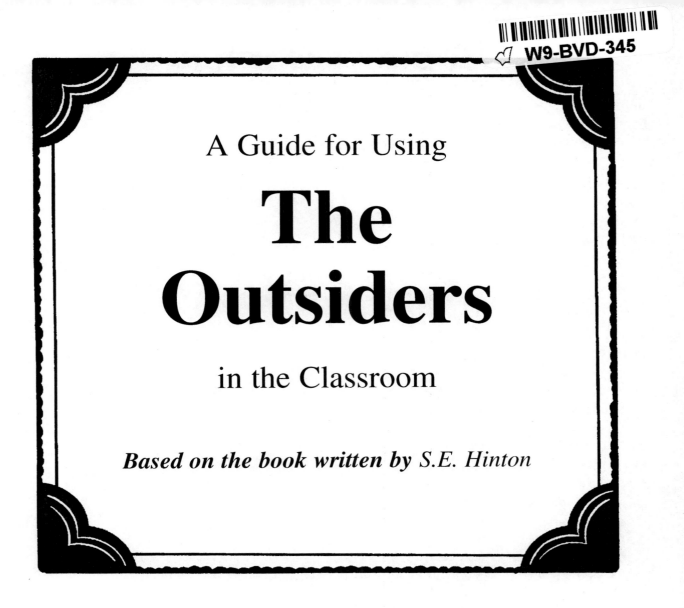

A Guide for Using

The Outsiders

in the Classroom

Based on the book written by S.E. Hinton

This guide written by John and Patty Carratello

Illustrated by Lynda Smythe

Teacher Created Materials

Teacher Created Materials, Inc.
6421 Industry Way
Westminster, CA 92683
www.teachercreated.com
©1992 *Teacher Created Materials*
Reprinted, 2003, a
Made in U.S.A.
ISBN 1-55734-406-X

Table of Contents

* Quiz Time!
* Hands-On Project— *"Tuff!"*
* Cooperative Learning Activity—*"We'll Make the Rules! "*
* Curriculum Connections—*Social Science: Groups*
* Into Your Life—*Reading Response Journals*

* Quiz Time!
* Hands-On Project—*The Hangout*
* Cooperative Learning Activity—*Resolving a Conflict*
* Curriculum Connections—*Music: Preferences*
* Into Your Life—*Dilemmas*

* Quiz Time!
* Hands-On Project—*Picture Time!*
* Cooperative Learning Activity—*Council of War or Peace?*
* Curriculum Connections—*Poetry*
* Into Your Life—*Would You Be a Hero?*

* Quiz Time!
* Hands-On Project—*Acrobatics!*
* Cooperative Learning Activity—*Finding Common Ground*
* Curriculum Connections—*Math: Attitude Survey*
* Into Your Life—*Advice*

* Quiz Time!
* Hands-On Project—*Sunsets*
* Cooperative Learning Activity—*Today's Problems*
* Curriculum Connections—*Psychology: Gangs*
* Into Your Life—*One Page . . .*

Introduction

A good book can touch our lives like a good friend. Within its pages are words and characters that can inspire us to achieve our highest ideals. We can turn to it for companionship, recreation, comfort, and guidance. It also gives us a cherished story to hold in our hearts forever.

In Literature Units, great care has been taken to select books that are sure to become good friends!

Teachers who use this literature unit will find the following features to supplement their own valuable ideas.

- Sample Lesson Plans
- Pre-reading Activities
- A Biographical Sketch and Picture of the Author
- A Book Summary
- Vocabulary Lists and Suggested Vocabulary Activities
- Chapters grouped for study, with each section including:
    - *—quizzes*
    - *—hands-on projects*
    - *—cooperative learning activities*
    - *—cross-curriculum connections*
    - *—extensions into the reader's own life*
- Post-reading Activities
- Book Report Ideas
- Research Ideas and/or Literary Terms Activities
- A Culminating Activity
- Three Different Options for Unit Tests
- Bibliography
- Answer Key

We are confident that this unit will be a valuable addition to your planning, and hope that as you use our ideas, your students will increase the circle of "friends" that they can have in books!

Sample Lesson Plan

Each of the lessons suggested below can take from one to several days to complete.

LESSON 1
- Introduce and complete some or all of the pre-reading activities found on page 5.
- Read "About the Author" with your students. (page 6)
- Read the book summary with your students. (page 7)
- Introduce literary terms activities to be completed throughout the unit. (page 37)
- Introduce the vocabulary list for SECTION 1. (page 8) Ask students to find definitions.

LESSON 2
- Read Chapters 1 and 2. As you read, place the vocabulary words in the context of the story and discuss their meanings.
- Choose a vocabulary activity. (page 9)
- Complete the plot summaries for chapters. (page 37)
- Make a "Tuff!" collage or montage. (page 11)
- Develop ideas and rules for living without parents. (page 12)
- Discuss the book in terms of social science. (page 13)
- Begin "Reading Response Journals." (page 14)
- Administer the SECTION 1 quiz. (page 10)
- Introduce the vocabulary list for SECTION 2. (page 8) Ask students to find definitions.

LESSON 3
- Read Chapters 3 and 4. Place the vocabulary words in context and discuss their meanings.
- Choose a vocabulary activity. (page 9)
- Complete the plot summaries for chapters. (page 37)
- Design the ideal hideout. (page 16)
- Discuss and practice the techniques of conflict resolution. (page 17)
- Discuss the book in terms of music. (page 18)
- When faced with dilemmas, make choices. (page 19)
- Administer SECTION 2 quiz. (page 15)
- Introduce the vocabulary list for SECTION 3. (page 8) Ask students to find definitions.

LESSON 4
- Read Chapters 5, 6, and 7. Place the vocabulary words in context and discuss their meanings.
- Choose a vocabulary activity. (page 9)
- Complete the plot summaries for chapters. (page 37)
- Try on different hairstyles! (page 21)
- Stage a council of war and/or a council of peace. (page 22)

- Discuss the book in terms of poetry. (page 23)
- Determine heroic qualities and heroic aptitude. (page 24)
- Administer SECTION 3 quiz. (page 20)
- Introduce the vocabulary list for SECTION 4. (page 8) Ask students to find definitions.

LESSON 5
- Read Chapters 8 and 9. Place the vocabulary words in context and discuss their meanings.
- Choose a vocabulary activity. (page 9)
- Complete the plot summaries for chapters. (page 37)
- Learn and practice simple acrobatics. (page 26)
- Work together to make parts a whole. (page 27)
- Discuss the book in terms of math. (page 28)
- Determine which advice Ponyboy receives is best for you. (page 29)
- Administer SECTION 4 quiz. (page 25)
- Introduce the vocabulary list for SECTION 5. (page 8) Ask students to find definitions.

LESSON 6
- Read Chapters 10, 11, and 12. Place the vocabulary words in context and discuss their meanings.
- Choose a vocabulary activity. (page 9)
- Complete the plot summaries for chapters. (page 37)
- Create sunsets. (page 31)
- Determine and rank problems facing youth today. (page 32)
- Discuss the book in terms of psychology. (page 33)
- Begin a page for your "composition". (page 34)
- Administer SECTION 5 quiz. (page 30)

LESSON 7
- Discuss any questions your students may have about the story. (page 35)
- Assign book report projects and review literary terms activities. (pages 36 and 37)
- Begin work on a culminating activity. (pages 38 through 41)

LESSON 8
- Administer one, two, and/or three unit tests. (pages 42, 43, and 44)
- Discuss the test answers and possibilities.
- Discuss the students' enjoyment of the book.
- Provide a list of related reading for your students. (page 45)

Before the Book

Before you begin reading *The Outsiders* with your students, do some pre-reading activities to stimulate interest and enhance comprehension. Here are some activities that might work well in your class.

1. Predict what the story might be about just by hearing the title.

2. Predict what the story might be about just by looking at the cover illustration.

3. Discuss other books by S.E. Hinton that students may have heard about or read, or movies they may have seen that have been based on her books.

4. Answer these questions:

   • Are you interested in:
     —stories told from the point of view of someone who is near your own age?
     —stories filled with dramatic action?
     —stories about two groups of people that have a conflict between them similar to a conflict you or someone you know might have?
     —stories which involve special friendships?

   • Would you ever:
     —join a gang?
     —be able to live in a household without parents, with only your older brothers to take care of you?
     —get in a physical fight to "handle" a problem?
     —run away with a close friend who had killed someone?
     —enjoy a sunrise or sunset with a friend?
     —stand up for what you think is right, even though all those around you don't agree?
     —write a book about your experiences?

   • Have you ever been so scared you wanted to hide?

   Describe your experience in detail.

5. Work in groups or as a class to create your own "gang conflict" story.

About the Author

Susan Eloise Hinton was born on July 22, 1948 in Tulsa, Oklahoma, where she continues to live today. Early in her life she wanted to be a cowboy or a writer, and her avid reading helped her toward one of these goals. Ms. Hinton says, "I started reading about the same time everyone else did, and began to write a short time later. The major influence on my writing has been my reading. I read everything, including Comet cans and coffee labels. Reading taught me sentence structure, paragraphing, how to build a chapter. Strangely enough, it never taught me spelling."[1]

According to her, it was her inability to spell that contributed to a D grade in Creative Writing when she was a junior at Will Rogers High School in Tulsa. It was during this same year that she finished a realistic book of fiction for teenagers. This book, *The Outsiders*, created a revolution in the writing of young adult novels upon its publication in 1967. For in this novel, Hinton portrayed a world realistic for many teenagers, filled with peer pressure, gang violence, social status, and parental abuse. It gave young people, used to stories of carefree innocents busy readying themselves for the big prom date, a dose of reality.

Susan Eloise Hinton became S.E. Hinton when *The Outsiders* was published. The concern was that boys might not want to read a book about gang life if they knew it was written by a girl. But she did know about gang life. Susan based her writing on her experiences with "greasers" and "socs" (pronounced soshes) in Tulsa. The characters she wrote about in *The Outsiders* are composites of the greasers and socs she knew, with some of herself mixed in. Although never a member of either group, she was able to represent both sides realistically in her story.

Because of her success as a novelist, she was able to go to the University of Tulsa, where she met her future husband, David Inhofe. In 1970, she graduated with a degree in education and, with David's encouragement, finished her second book, *That Was Then, This Is Now*, in 1971. *Rumble Fish* was written in 1975 and *Tex* in 1979. In 1983, David and Susan had a son, Nicholas. *Taming the Star Runner* was published in 1988.

Hinton's books have won numerous awards throughout the years, and major motion pictures have been made of *The Outsiders; That Was Then, This Is Now; Rumble Fish*; and *Tex*. Her success can be attributed to the realism of the characters who people her books. They come to life in the richness of her characterizations which are sincere, honest, and believable. "I'm a character writer. Some writers are plot writers.... I have to begin with people. I always know my characters, exactly what they look like, their birthdays, what they like for breakfast. It doesn't matter if these things appear in the book. I still have to know. My characters are fictional. I get ideas from real people, sometimes, but my characters always exist only in my head.... Those characters are as real to me as anyone else in my life, so much so that if I ran into one of them at the laundry, I wouldn't be all that surprised."[2]

[1] as quoted in "Advice from a Penwoman" *Seventeen*, November, 1981
[2] as quoted in "Notes from Delacorte Press for Books for Young Readers" *Delacorte Press*, winter, 1979/spring, 1980

The Outsiders
by S.E. Hinton
(Delacorte Press, 1967)

The east side of town shapes the life of fourteen-year-old Ponyboy Curtis. It's where he lives and where his friends are. Together they are the Greasers, a local gang with a tough reputation and a uniform of long oiled hair, blue jeans, and t-shirts. The Greasers have a big problem, however. Their problem is the rival gang from the town's west side. The Socials, or Socs, as they are called, sport fancy cars, wear madras shirts, and party wildly. And, their favorite pastime is ganging up on lone Greasers. One such jumping begins the action of *The Outsiders*.

While walking home alone from the movies, Ponyboy is jumped, teased, and intimidated by a group of rowdy Socs, and would have been severely beaten had it not been for the intervention of his Greaser buddies. But the Socs continue the fight again the next night. They believe that Greasers have picked up their girlfriends and are now bent on revenge. Completely drunk, they corner Johnny and Ponyboy in the park and hold Ponyboy's head under water. Johnny, fearing for his friend's life, knives one of the Socs and kills him. The other Socs flee. The young Greasers are terrified and turn to Dally, the streetwise, hood-like member of the gang, for help. He suggests they hide out for a while in the country outside of town.

For five days they hide, keeping each other company with the reading of *Gone With the Wind*, playing cards, and sharing the beauty of the sunrise. When Dally comes to bring them supplies and news from home about the impending all-out rumble between the Greasers and the Socs, Johnny decides to turn himself in. As they drive by the abandoned church in which they were hiding, they see it engulfed in flames, stop to investigate, and hear the cries of children who have been trapped inside. The three boys make a gallant effort to save the children and each other. They succeed and are recognized as heroes.

Their heroic behavior and the Socs' testimony that the murder was self-defense practically insure their acquittal. Johnny, however, seriously injured in the fire, is close to death. To fight for their friend and their identities, Ponyboy and Dally join with the other Greasers in the big rumble and emerge "victorious." The two boys rush to the hospital to tell Johnny the news. But moments after their arrival, Johnny dies, and Dally, despondent over the death of his friend, makes himself a target for the police and is gunned down. Ponyboy soon collapses, falling ill for days. When he comes out of his illness and depression, he begins to make some sense of the world in which he lives, and vows to make it better by telling his story in a book— *The Outsiders*.

Vocabulary Lists

On this page are vocabulary lists which correspond to each sectional grouping of chapters. Vocabulary activity ideas can be found on page 9 of this book.

SECTION 1

acquired	reckless
clammy	roguishly
disgrace	sagely
gingerly	sarcastically
glaring	sensitive
incidentally	stalked
incredulous	stocky
irresistibly	sympathetic
nonchalantly	unfathomable
rarities	

SECTION 2

apprehensive	premonition
avoiding	quavered
bewildering	quivering
bleak	rave
contemptuously	resignedly
defiance	ruefully sassy
dumbfounded	sophisticated
gallantly	unceasingly
groggy ornery	winced
passionately	

SECTION 3

aghast	imploringly
apparently	indignant
bewilderment	individual
contemptuously	mimicking
conviction	radiates
desperately	stunned
doggedly	subsides
eluded hue	sullenly vital
hysterics	wistfully

SECTION 4

abruptly	grimacing
acrobatics	leery
agony	miniature
aimlessly	mock numbly
awed clenching	reformatory
contempt	static
debating	stifled
disgusted	superiority
environment	underprivileged

SECTION 5

Acquitted	hazy idolized
circumstances	stupor vaguely
concussion	veered
daze delirious	
flinching	

Vocabulary Activity Ideas

You can help your students learn and retain the vocabulary in *The Outsiders* by providing them with interesting vocabulary activities. Here are a few ideas to try.

- ❑ People of all ages like to make and solve puzzles. Ask your students to make their own **Crossword Puzzles** or **Wordsearch Puzzles** using the vocabulary words from the story.

- ❑ Challenge your students to a **Vocabulary Bee**. This is similar to a spelling bee, but in addition to spelling each word correctly, the game participants must correctly define the words as well.

- ❑ Play **Vocabulary Concentration**. The goal of this game is to match vocabulary words with their definitions. Divide the class into groups of 2-5 students. Have students make two sets of cards the same size and color. On one set have them write the vocabulary words. On the second set have them write the definitions. All cards are mixed together and placed face down on a table. A player picks two cards. If the pair matches the word with its definition, the player keeps the cards and takes another turn. If the cards don't match, they are returned to their places face down to the table, and another player takes a turn. Players must concentrate to remember the locations of words and their definitions. The game continues until all matches have been made. This is an ideal activity for free exploration time.

- ❑ Have your students practice their writing skills by creating sentences and paragraphs in which multiple vocabulary words are used correctly. Ask them to share their **Compact Vocabulary** sentences and paragraphs with the class.

- ❑ Play **Hangman**, using the definition as a clue. This is a good activity to be played in partners.

- ❑ Challenge your students to use a specific vocabulary word from the story at least **10 Times In One Day**. They must keep a record of when, how, and why the word was used.

- ❑ As a group activity, have students work together to create an **Illustrated Dictionary** of the vocabulary words.

- ❑ Play **20 Clues** with the entire class. In this game, one student selects a vocabulary word and gives clues about this word, one by one, until someone in the class can guess the word.

- ❑ Play **Vocabulary Charades**. In this game, vocabulary words are acted out.

  You probably have many more ideas to add to this list. Try them. See if experiencing vocabulary on a personal level increases your students' vocabulary interest and retention!

Quiz Time!

1. On the back of this paper, write a one paragraph summary of the major events in each chapter of this section. Then complete the rest of the questions on this page.

2. What happens to Ponyboy on his way home from the movies?

   _____

   _____

3. Briefly describe the conflict between the Greasers and the Socs.

   _____

   _____

4. What happened to the Curtis brothers' parents?

   _____

   _____

5. How is Ponyboy different from the rest of the Greasers?

   _____

   _____

6. In one well-written sentence, characterize Darry.

   _____

   _____

7. In one well-written sentence, characterize Sodapop.

   _____

   _____

8. List the Greasers who are at the movies "with" Cherry and Marcia.

   _____   _____   _____   _____

9. What does Ponyboy tell Cherry while standing in line for popcorn?

   _____

   _____

10. On the back of this paper, explain what Cherry Valance means when she says, "Things are rough all over."

Tuff!

Ponyboy explains the meanings of a few words Greasers use so that we, as readers, will know exactly what he means when he uses them.

> "*Tough* and *tuff* are two different words. *Tough* is the same as rough; *tuff* means cool, sharp—like a tuff-looking Mustang or a tuff record. In our neighborhood both are compliments."

What do you think is *tuff*? Is it a particular haircut or style of clothing? Is it a car, bicycle, or motorcycle? Are your ideas of *tuff* different than the ideas of others you know?

For this project, make a collage or montage of what is *tuff*.

Suggested Material:

- a large piece of posterboard for your display
- consumable magazines, newspapers, and other print media for *tuff* "cut-outs" to glue on your display
- fabric samples of *tuff* materials
- jewelry (inexpensive samples, please!)
- album jackets or jacket copies of *tuff* musicians
- nail polish and lipstick samples
- titles of *tuff* books, videos, or movies
- lists or pictures of *tuff* people in your life
- any other *tuff*, appropriate ideas you would like to include
- photographs

When you have finished your display, share it with the class. Do your classmates and teacher have similar ideas of *tuff*?

We'll Make the Rules!

Ponyboy, Sodapop, and Darry Curtis live without their parents. As you remember from your reading, Mr. and Mrs. Curtis were killed in an automobile accident. The three boys have been told they can stay together as long as they stay out of trouble.

It would be tragic to lose your parents. But what if your parents decided to leave you alone for a month while they traveled? In the very unlikely event that this would happen, could you get along without them?

For this activity, you will need to work in a cooperative learning group of three or four people. You will be required to do the following things:

- Assign jobs to each group member. Some jobs must be household jobs, others must supply income. Each group member must have both a household and an income job.

- Plan the meals you would eat in a typical week (7 days) for breakfast, lunch, and dinner. Decide on the responsibilities for each meal.

- Determine what you will do for transportation, as none of you can drive legally.

- Determine a set of "house" rules, including such things as "lights out," "visiting hours," "conflict management," and "television time." Make your list as long as you think necessary.

- Plan a schedule of school-night and weekend night activities. Decide how homework will be handled efficiently.

- Determine the procedure you will follow in an emergency. You cannot call your parents.

- Anticipate the problems you might have without adult supervision. Plan ahead with ways you could handle these problems.

Add any other ideas you and your group have. Perhaps you want to draft a letter to your parents to let them know how you are doing!

Social Science: Groups

The conflict between the Greasers and the Socs is one that is repeated throughout the world, only with different names. In society, there are those who are rich who look down upon and ridicule those who are poor. There are those who are poor who are envious of those who are rich and do things to try to "get back." In *The Outsiders*, told from the point of view of Ponyboy Curtis, Socs started conflicts with the Greasers. Perhaps they wanted other teenagers to know who was in control. Maybe they just did it for the kind of "kicks" money can't buy. Whatever the reason, the struggle the Greasers experienced was real. Other people, those in real life we know or read about, experience such struggle, too.

As a class project, prepare a profile of the teenage social groups in your school or town. Include items such as the following in your report.

- What types of different social groups exist in your school or town?

- What characteristics make up the people in each group? Here are some ideas:
    —racial background
    —religious background
    —athletic ability
    —money
    —physical appearance
    —intelligence
    —personal habits
    —neighborhoods
    —past history

- How do people in these different groups interact within their own groups?

- How do groups interact with other groups?

- Are there fights that frequently occur among members of different groups? If so, what kind of fights are there? Where do the fights occur? How are they resolved?

- What changes because of the fighting?

- Are there important reasons to be in a social group? If so, what are the reasons?

- Do members join groups willingly?

- Are any of the groups dangerous?

- Are any of the groups helpful?

Reading Response Journals

One great way to insure that the reading of *The Outsiders* touches each student in a personal way is to include the use of Reading Response Journals in your plans. In these journals, students can be encouraged to respond to the story in a number of ways. Here are a few ideas.

- Ask students to create a journal for *The Outsiders*. Initially, just have them assemble lined and un-lined three-holed paper in a brad-fastened "book," with a blank page for the journal's cover. As they read the story, they may draw a design on the cover that helps tell the story for them.

- Tell them that the purpose of the journal is to record their thoughts, ideas, observations, and questions as they read *The Outsiders*.

- Provide students with, or ask them to suggest, topics from the story that would stimulate writing.

  Here are a few examples from the chapters in SECTION 1.

  — When Ponyboy left the movie theater and was jumped by the Socs, he was deeply afraid.

      Describe the kinds of fears you have felt.

  — Greasers and Socs were different from each other, and this difference caused many fights.

    How would you feel if you were a Greaser? How would you feel if you were a Soc?

- After the reading of each chapter, students can write one or more new things they learned in the chapter.

- Ask students to draw their responses to certain events or characters in the story, using the blank pages in their journals.

- Tell students that they may use their journals to record "diary-type" responses that they may want to enter.

- Encourage students to bring their journal ideas to life! Ideas generated from their journal writing can be used to create plays, debates, stories, songs, and art displays.

- Allow students time to write in their journals daily.

- Explain to the students that their Reading Response Journals can be evaluated in a number of ways. Here are a few ideas.

  — Personal reflections will be read by the teacher, but no corrections or letter grades will be assigned. Credit is given for effort, and all students who sincerely try will be awarded credit. If a "grade" is desired for this type of entry, you could grade according to the number of journal entries for the number of journal assignments. For example, if five journal assignments were made and the student conscientiously completes all five, then he or she should receive an "A."

  — Nonjudgmental teacher responses should be made as you read the journals to let the students know that you are reading and enjoying their journals. Here are some types of responses that will please your journal writers and encourage them to write more.

      "You have really found what's important in the story!"

      "WOW! This is interesting stuff!"

      "You write so clearly, I almost feel as if I am there!"

      "You seem to be able to learn from this book and apply what you learn to your life!"

      "If you feel comfortable doing so, I'd like you to share your idea with the class. They will enjoy what you've written!"

If you would like to grade student writing for form and content, ask the students to select one of their entries and "edit it" according to the writing process.

Quiz Time!

1. On the back of this paper, write a one paragraph summary of the major events that happen in each of the chapters in this section. Then complete the rest of the questions on this page.

2. What does Cherry say is the real separation between the Socs and the Greasers?

3. Who is Mickey Mouse and why is he so important in Sodapop's life?

4. Why does Ponyboy remind Cherry that they both watch the same sunsets?

5. Why is Ponyboy surprised when Cherry tells him with whom she might be likely to fall in love?

6. Explain Ponyboy's motivation for running away.

7. What did the Socs do to make Johnny kill Bob?

8. In one well-written sentence, characterize Dally.

9. What does Dally give Ponyboy and Johnny to take with them to Windrixville?

10. How long do you think the boys will be able to hide out at the church? Why?

The Hangout

The Socs party at the river bottom, the Greasers hang out at the vacant lot, and the Shepard outfit congregates in the alleys down by the tracks. Each group has a place they call their own.

Do you have a hangout? If so, what does it look like? If not, what kind of place would you like to have to meet with your friends?

- Where would it be?

- What would it look like?

- Is it close to where you live?

- Would it be easily accessible to others?

- Would it protect you in the rain?

- Would you build it or does it already exist?

- Would it appeal to other groups, too?

- What are some of its special features?

- Will it be standing in ten years?

Using three-dimensional material, such as clay, cardboard, plastic figures, sticks, rocks, or sand, reproduce or design the perfect hangout for you and your special friends. Affix your creation to a lightweight board for portability. You may work by yourself or with one or two partners. When you have finished, share your ideal place with the others in your class.

Resolving a Conflict

The Greasers and the Socs may have been able to live more harmoniously if they knew and applied some simple techniques of conflict management. Instead of beating a face with a ring-covered hand, threatening an opponent with a broken bottle, or throwing a soda in someone's face, the angry ones might have resolved their problems peacefully.

Work in small groups to resolve these conflicts that occurred in *The Outsiders* by using one or more of the management techniques suggested below. Dramatize at least one of your group's ideas for peaceful resolution for the class.

1. Darry is angry with his brother Ponyboy because he is two hours late. Darry is tempted to hit him for the first time.

2. Johnny and Ponyboy are minding their own business late at night in the park. A group of drunken Socs comes after them.

3. Dally makes Cherry mad. When he offers her a soda, she is tempted to throw it in his face.

1. **SAY YOU ARE SORRY**. Sometimes these words are the only thing the other person needs. Sometimes an explanation of why you are sorry will help, too.

2. **COUNT TO 10 (or 15 or 20!)** This gives you time to cool down a bit and a chance to think before you act. Think about the different choices you have in the situation. Think about the consequences of the different actions you could take. Decide which choice of action is the best for you.

3. **TAKE TURNS TELLING EACH SIDE OF THE PROBLEM**. Let the other person go first. Let the person finish all he or she has to say. Then you take your turn. You might start out by saying something like, "Why are you mad?"

4. **HAVE ANOTHER PERSON YOU BOTH RESPECT HELP YOU SETTLE IT**. Another person can often help you both see the other person's point of view.

5. **MAKE A JOKE ABOUT THE SITUATION,** so the other person will not take the conflict so seriously. Laughter eases many tensions.

6. **WALK AWAY!** This is sometimes hard to do, especially if other people are watching to see what you will do.

7. **STAY OUT OF TROUBLE.** Remember, the best way to keep a conflict from happening is to avoid it in the first place. Be aware of how your actions might look to others. Be careful not to hurt people's feelings or embarrass them.

Music: Preferences

The Greasers like Elvis Presley, the Socs like the Beatles, and Buck Merril likes Hank Williams. Who do you like?

For this activity, your teacher will play you three recordings:

>   one by Elvis Presley

>   one by The Beatles

>   one by Hank Williams

Rate each selection on a 1 to 10 scale, with a 10 being what you enjoy most. After you have finished your individual ratings, graph the class scores. Include your teacher's score, too.

Who emerges as the favorite recording artist in your class?

ELVIS PRESLEY

song: _____

_____

ranking: _____

THE BEATLES

song: _____

_____

ranking: _____

HANK WILLIAMS, SR.

song: _____

_____

ranking: _____

Dilemmas

Throughout our lives, we are faced with choices. Sometimes the choices we make are the right ones, and we experience success. At other times, the choices we make may be ones that do not give us positive experiences, and we learn from the mistakes we have made.

From time to time, we are faced with choices that are not desirable. These are called dilemmas. We have to make a decision based on our best judgment, knowing that the outcome may not be pleasant. It is one thing to be faced with a choice between strawberry or chocolate ice cream. It is quite another to be faced with a choice between standing up to a bully or running to hide.

The characters in *The Outsiders* faced many dilemmas. Few choices were clear-cut and easy for them to make. Their lives would have been quite simple if their only choices involved ice cream!

For this activity, work with a partner. Cut and stack the "dilemma" cards found on this page and add some more of your own. Place the stack between you and take turns drawing the cards. When you draw a card, read the situation, formulate a choice, and explain your choice to your partner. Your partner may then ask you questions so he or she can more clearly understand the choice you have made.

A teenager with a knife approaches you and demands you give him or her your new bicycle. Should you: 1. scream loudly? 2. try to race away? 3. stand up to him or her and say no? 4. other?	Your mother and father trust you not to have friends over while they are out. A very attractive person has asked to come over. Should you: 1. say yes? 2. ask the person to come when your parents return? 3. ask your parent to make an exception to the rule? 4. other?
The group you hang around with has been teasing a boy at school. The boy is hurting. Your group expects you to go along with teasing or be kicked out of the group. Should you: 1. tease the boy to stay in the group? 2. refuse to tease and be kicked out? 3. tease, and later tell the boy you're sorry? 4. other?	Your best friend committed a shoplifting crime. You are the only person who knows. Should you: 1. encourage your friend to turn himself or herself in? 2. remain silent? 3. make arrangements with the store manager to pay back the store to get your friend off the hook? 4. other?

Quiz Time!

1. On the back of this paper, write a one paragraph summary of the major events that happen in each of the chapters of this section. Then, complete the rest of the questions on this page.

2. Why is Ponyboy's hair so important to him? _____

_____

_____

3. On the back of this paper, explain the meaning of the poem, "Nothing Gold Can Stay," from Chapter 5.

4. When Dally comes to the abandoned church, he brings Ponyboy a letter from Sodapop. Describe the contents of the letter.

_____

_____

5. Who is the spy for the Greasers?_____

6. Why does Johnny decide to turn himself in?

_____

_____

7. In one well-written sentence, characterize Dally's relationship with Johnny.

_____

_____

8. What do Johnny and Ponyboy do when they know the children are in the church? Are they scared?

_____

_____

9. What does the doctor say will happen to Johnny?

_____

_____

10. What Soc wants to talk to Ponyboy? Why?

_____

_____

Picture Time!

New haircuts, a little bleach, and oil-free hair changed the way Ponyboy and Johnny looked. They were both quite startled at their "new look."

Have you ever wondered how you would look with a different hair style or hair color?

For this activity you will need your small school wallet picture. Color the hair and clothes in the "pictures" below. Then, carefully cut out the "faceless" portion and each frame. Place your school picture behind each frame and see the transformation! Do you like the new you?

Council of War or Peace?

The Greasers and the Socs held a "War Council" to settle the tension between them "once and for all."

Suppose you were in on this "War Council." Knowing what you know about the characters in *The Outsiders*, do you think you could have an impact and change the council of war into a council of peace?

For this activity, you will need to work in groups of four to twelve. Select a group member to play the part of one of the characters on this list. Be sure to assign someone to each name with an asterisk (*). For the sake of this exercise, pretend that Bob is not dead and Johnny is not in the hospital.

- Dallas   Randy
- Bob   Johnny
- Cherry   Two-Bit
- Ponyboy   Darry
- Sodapop   Tim Shephard
- Sandy   Marcia

Practice interacting as if you really are the character you have been assigned to play. (Remember to keep your actions and words appropriate for the classroom!)

Working together, plan two role-playing situations. In one situation, make the outcome "war." In the second situation, make the outcome "peace."

Perform your dramas for the rest of the class.

Poetry

Robert Frost's "Nothing Gold Can Stay" plays a prominent role in the story of *The Outsiders*. Johnny and Ponyboy are both touched by a spectacular sunrise, and Frost's words say what the boys cannot.

Poetry captures a variety of feelings. You have had the opportunity to read poetry throughout your life, and have probably been touched by some poems you have read.

For this activity, you will be asked to do some or all of the following things:

- Read five other poems by Robert Frost.

- Read five poems by an author of your choice.

- Read ten poems of your choice by ten authors, different from Frost and the one you have chosen above.

- Read five of your favorite poems to someone in your family.

- Copy three favorite poems neatly onto notecards to give as gifts.

- Memorize a favorite poem and recite it for the class.

- Participate in the making of a "Favorite Poems" bulletin board display.

- Write your own poem about the sunrise.

- Write five other original poems.

- Using your best writing, copy your favorite original poem on a piece of parchment paper and frame it.

Would You Be a Hero?

There are many kinds of heroes. It is difficult to predict how an individual might react in a situation where risking one's life may save another's.

Think about what your response might be to the following situations and questions.

Situation:

Randy is very curious about Ponyboy's display of heroism when he saved the children from the burning church. He doesn't believe he would have done the same thing.

" 'I wouldn't have. I would have let those kids burn to death.' " Ponyboy counters with,

" 'You might not have. You might have done the same thing.' " Ponyboy goes on to say,

" 'My friend over there wouldn't have done it. Maybe you would have done the same thing, maybe a friend of yours wouldn't have. It's the individual.' "

Questions:

1.   Would you have saved the children in the burning church? On the back of this paper, list the reasons why you think you might have saved the kids and the reasons you think you might not have saved them.

2.   Johnny, Ponyboy, and Dallas were heroes. What makes them heroes?

   _____

   _____

   _____

3.   Name four people in your life that have the capacity to become the type of heroes that Ponyboy, Johnny, and Dallas were in *The Outsiders*.

   _____   _____

   _____   _____

4.   What is your definition of a hero?

   _____

   _____

5.   By your definition, are you heroic? Explain your answer on the back of this paper..

Quiz Time!

1. On the back of this paper, write a one paragraph summary of the major events that happen in each of the chapters in this section. Then, complete the questions on the rest of this page.

2. Explain Ponyboy's words when he visits Johnny in the hospital: "I figured that Southern gentlemen had nothing on Johnny Cade."

    _____

    _____

3. What is Johnny's reaction when the nurse tells him that his mother is at the hospital to see him?

    _____

    _____

4. What reason does Cherry give Ponyboy for not going to see Johnny in the hospital?

    _____

    _____

5. In one well-written sentence, describe the mood at the Curtis house just before the rumble.

    _____

    _____

6. Ponyboy feels the only reason to fight is self-defense. According to his survey, why do these others fight?

    Darry _____   Soda _____

    Two-Bit _____   Steve _____

7. Who comes late to the rumble? _____ What effect does his late entrance have?

    _____

    _____

8. What kind of weapons do the Greasers and Socs use in the rumble?

    _____

    _____

9. Where does Dally take Ponyboy after the rumble?

    _____

10. What are Johnny's last words? _____

Acrobatics!

Darry taught the boys all he learned from an acrobatics class. As a result, they were quite adept at doing cartwheels, handsprings, flips, and flying somersaults.

Can you walk on your hands, do somersaults, and turn cartwheels?

For this "hands-on" activity, you will get the chance to learn, practice, and perform some simple acrobatics!

Walking On Your Hands

1. Find a safe, flat, soft surface.

2. Stand with your feet together.

3. Put your arms above your head with your hands open and fingers spread.

4. Put one foot in front of you and, as you do, shift your weight forward to that foot.

5. As you shift your weight, start bending quickly from the waist, with you arms extended outward.

6. As your palms begin to touch the ground in front of you, start shifting your weight to your palms.

7. Keeping your elbows "locked," kick both your feet upward, leading with your back foot.

8. Quickly straighten your body, until you are able to stand on your hands.

9. Once you have gotten into a hand stand, try to "walk" with your hands.

Somersault (basic)

1. Get into a squat position, with feet together, your knees even with your shoulders, your arms touching the outside of your legs, and your hands, with your fingers spread, on the ground, just past your knees.

2. Roll forward, trying to touch your chin to your chest, and supporting most of your body weight with your arms.

3. Stop when your feet or your legs touch the ground.

Cartwheel

Can you write directions for turning a cartwheel? Try it! After you have done your best, read your directions to a friend, family member, or classmate. Can he or she follow your directions and turn a cartwheel?

After you have learned and practiced handwalks, somersaults, and cartwheels, perform what you can do for your classmates, your family, or a friend!

Finding Common Ground

The Greasers and the Socs lived in two separate "worlds," unlikely to ever see the need to live harmoniously together. No one was seen as an individual by the members of the opposing gang, just "lumped" into the category of Greaser or Soc and left there. Ponyboy, Johnny, Two-Bit, Cherry, Marcia, and Randy were quite surprised to discover that members of rival groups could be individuals with hopes, fears, humor, and pain.

Suppose they had the opportunity and the desire to learn about each other sooner. Do you think the tragedies that filled *The Outsiders* could have been avoided? Perhaps, if the teachers at Ponyboy's high school had grouped their students so that people who were different could see they had similarities, tension between the gangs could have lessened.

Here is a method to group students for activities in a classroom. Duplicate a puzzle form for every four students in your classroom. (Puzzle forms can be found on page 48.)

- Write a student's name on each puzzle piece. You may wish to form heterogeneous groups or simply write the names in alphabetical order.

- Laminate the puzzles for durability.

- Cut apart the puzzle pieces and mix all of them together.

- Distribute a piece to each class member.

- Ask students to move about the classroom trying to find their "puzzle mates."

Now that people have been grouped, complete an activity requiring the participation of each group member. Here are some ideas.

- Each group member has an object. The group must work together to make something whole out of their parts. (Sample objects: four toothpicks, a potato, yarn pieces, a plastic cup, three paper clips, a bar of soap, two rubber bands, a bell, etc.)

- Each group can develop a list of items upon which they agree. It can be a listing of things such as songs, performers, TV comedies, movies, spare-time activities, foods, or sports.

The Outsiders

Math: Attitude Survey

Ponyboy determines the reasons members of the Greasers fight. As you were reading his conclusions in Chapter 9, did you try to determine if and why you would fight?

As a class activity, take a survey of attitudes about fighting. Have each person write his/her name and mark each box that he/she believes to be an acceptable reason to fight. When you have completed your research using the data collection chart below, graph your results.

Reasons for Fighting

Class Member	Pride	Fun	Conformity	Hatred	Self-Defense	Other

28

Advice

Ponyboy receives two pieces of advice at the end of Chapter 9.

"I was crazy, you know that, kid? Crazy for wantin' Johnny to stay outa trouble, for not wantin' him to get hard. If he'd been like me he'd never have been in this mess. If he'd got smart like me he'd never have run into that church. That's what you get for helpin' people. Editorials in the paper and a lot of trouble…You'd better wise up, Pony…you get tough like me and you don't get hurt. You look out for yourself and nothin' can touch you."

— Dallas Winston

"Stay gold, Ponyboy. Stay gold . . ."

— Johnny Cade

Answer the following questions on a separate sheet of paper.

1. Which advisor do you think Ponyboy will be inclined to follow? Why?

2. Whose advice would you be more apt to follow? Why?

3. Can you defend the advice you did not choose in #2? Do your best to argue this point of view.

4. Which advice do you feel the majority of the people you know and have as friends would follow? Why?

5. In light of the events that happened up through Chapter 9, what new advice would you have given Ponyboy? Neatly write your advice in this box. Then, all class advice ideas can be cut out and displayed in the classroom.

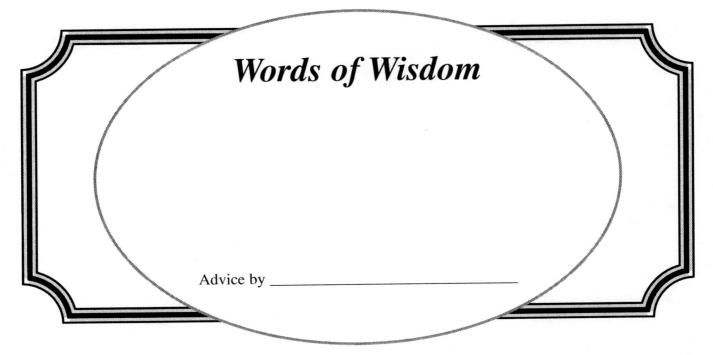

Words of Wisdom

Advice by _____

Quiz Time!

1. On the back of this page, write a one paragraph summary of the main events that happen in each of the chapters in this section. Then, complete the rest of the questions on this page.

2. Why can't Dally accept Johnny's death?

_____

_____

3. Does Dally want to die? Explain.

_____

_____

4. Why does Ponyboy collapse the night of the rumble?

_____

_____

5. What does Johnny give to the nurse for Ponyboy?

_____

_____

6. What thoughts are triggered in Ponyboy's mind when he sees Bob in the yearbook?

_____

_____

7. Who does Ponyboy tell Randy was the person who killed Bob?

_____

8. What does Ponyboy do with the broken bottle glass that makes Two-Bit know that Ponyboy will not get tough?

_____

_____

9. In the letter Johnny writes Ponyboy, what does he ask Ponyboy to tell Dally?

_____

_____

10. What is the subject of Ponyboy's theme for English class?

_____

Sunsets

Ponyboy and Cherry both realize that people, no matter how different, can see and appreciate the same sunset. This hands-on activity gives you a chance to create a sunset for yourself and others to enjoy!

Create a sunset out of any suitable art materials. Here are some ideas.

- colored sand
- small beads
- grated fruit peel or fruit peel strips
- dried leaves and blossoms of flowers
- herbs and spices
- colored pasta
- fabric scraps
- colored pencils
- watercolors
- chalk
- modeling clay
- plastic strips
- tiny construction paper squares
- tissue paper
- fingerpaint
- scratch board

- colored eggshells
- yarn
- ribbon
- wrapping paper
- feathers
- colored birdseed
- pudding paint
- shredded Easter grass
- beans
- glitter
- marking pens
- colored popcorn
- crayons
- table salt and rock salt
- paint

Here are two of these ideas described in detail.

Eggshell Sunset

- Wash and dry eggshell pieces.
- Prepare eggshell dye: ½ cup water, ½ teaspoon vinegar, a few drops of selected food color. You may also use commercially-made egg dye.
- Place the eggshell pieces in various "sunset" colors for approximately 5 minutes or until desired color is reached.
- Remove eggshells from dye and let them dry on paper towels.
- Dribble glue on a sheet of construction paper.
- Arrange eggshells on the glue and let them dry.
- Admire your sunset and share it with others!

Salt Sunset

- Dribble glue all over white construction paper.
- Scatter approximately 1/4 cup of rock salt on the glue.
- Scatter approximately 1/4 cup of table salt on the glue.
- Sprinkle drops of food coloring over the salt mixture.
- Let your pictures dry.
- Watch the color seem to sparkle through the salt crystals.
- Admire your sunset and share it with others!

Today's Problems

In *The Outsiders*, the teenagers in the story faced realistic problems. Many of these problems face today's teenagers as well. Working in groups of three or four, brainstorm lists of problems that faced the characters in *The Outsiders*. Use a separate sheet of paper. Here are a few ideas to get you started.

alcohol abuse	teenage pregnancy
gang violence	search for self
parental neglect	peer pressure

Still working with the same group, circle the problems that you identified in *The Outsiders* that are very real problems for you or teenagers you know.

Next, add current teenage problems that haven't been mentioned in **The Outsiders**-based list.

As a group, select ten problems from your combined list that you feel are the most critical problems facing teenagers today. Write them down in the order of importance in the box below. (#1 is the most critical problem; #2 is second most critical, etc.)

The Ten Most Critical Problems Facing Teenagers Today

Group members: _____

_____

1. _____   6. _____

2. _____   7. _____

3. _____   8. _____

4. _____   9. _____

5. _____   10. _____

Share your list with the others in your class. How similar are your lists? Are there ways you can face or avoid these problems? Invite a counselor to your class to speak of ways to lessen the effect of these and similar problems in your life.

Psychology: Gangs

Many young people throughout the world are a part of gangs. Sometimes the gangs are "social" clubs, formed because people with the same interests like to get together and do the things they enjoy doing with others. Gangs may be created for protection, so a group of people who feel threatened in some way can band together to make a strong defense. Gangs can be a requirement of a geographic area, and if you don't belong to one, you are ostracized. Other times gangs are organized to commit criminal acts. Sometimes gangs are a reflection of style preferences, such as long hair, greasy hair, or no hair. Some gangs are based on ethnic background or religious belief. These are some of the more evident reasons for gang formation.

In *The Outsiders*, Greasers band together because of life on the East Side, low income, and greasy, long hair. Socs band together because of life on the West Side, high income, and well-maintained stylishness.

Many young people today are tempted or expected to become gang members. These gang members fight other gangs for the same reasons the Greasers and the Socs fought in *The Outsiders*. They are rivals and are expected to fight, especially if they are found on one another's turf.

Would you enjoy belonging to a gang? Why?

_____

_____

_____

_____

Determine one positive and one negative aspect of gang membership.

Positive:_____

_____

_____

Negative: _____

_____

_____

On the back of this paper, describe the gang activity that exists in your school or community, and determine its causes. If there is no gang activity in your school or community, determine the reasons gangs are absent.

One Page...

Ponyboy resolves to do something to make a difference to the hundreds of boys who live on "the wrong sides of cities," who "jumped at their shadows," and who "watched sunsets and looked at stars and ached for something better."

> *"Someone should tell their side of the story, and maybe people would understand then and wouldn't be so quick to judge a boy by the amount of hair oil he wore."*

He writes his story in the form of a composition for an English assignment. The result is the story of *The Outsiders*.

Have there been events in your life that have triggered the need to share with others? Make a few notes on these lines.

_____

_____

_____

_____

_____

_____

Read this list. See if you have felt strongly about any of these ideas.

- Someone you know dies a tragic and avoidable death.
- You see or experience the unfair treatment of one group of people.
- A special friendship gives you strength.
- Misunderstandings are a "way of life" in your family.
- A society in which money gives others the "right" to ridicule others is unfair.
- Money brings happiness.
- Too much money brings grief.
- Parents need to set limits for their children.
- Drug and/or alcohol abuse governs lives.
- You would give up your life for someone else.
- You wonder if other people your age feel the same as you do.

Select an idea that "triggers" the possibility of a story in your mind. Write the first page of that story. Chances are, if it is something you really care about, you won't be able to stop at one page! So, feel free to continue.

Any Questions?

When you finished reading *The Outsiders*, did you have some questions that were left unanswered? Write some of your questions here.

_____

_____

_____

Work in groups or by yourself to prepare possible answers for some or all of the questions you have asked above and those written below. When you have finished your predictions, share your ideas with the class.

* Do the Curtis boys have any relatives that could have helped them out when their parents died?
* Does Ponyboy's English teacher like his writing assignment?
* Does Sodapop ever find a horse he loves as much as Mickey Mouse?
* Do Two-Bit and Marcia date?
* Do the Greasers and Socs continue fighting with each other?
* Does Ponyboy go to college?
* Does Darry ever go to college?
* How will Ponyboy's experiences with Socs affect his attitude toward other Socs?
* Do Ponyboy and Cherry ever look at sunsets together?
* Do Johnny's parents see the other Greasers after Johnny's death?
* Does Ponyboy ever share Johnny's message about staying gold with anyone else?
* Will Ponyboy ever live in the country?
* Do the people of Windrixville ever get in touch with Ponyboy again?
* Does the court allow the Curtis brothers to stay together?
* Do Ponyboy's experience and intellect ever allow him to become friends with people who are not Greasers?
* Do you think that the school's principal and teachers ever do anything to combat the friction between the Socs and the Greasers?
* Do you think what happens in *The Outsiders* is typical or atypical of what happens in most schools today?
* What happens to Sodapop and Sandy?
* Do Paul and Darry ever see each other again and talk about the changes in their lives since high school graduation?
* Does Randy ever jump a Greaser again?
* Does Darry remain a roofer, Sodapop a gas station attendant, and Ponyboy a writer during their adult lives?
* What would this story have been like if told from another point of view, such as the view of Sodapop, Bob, Cherry, Johnny, Dallas, Mr. and Mrs. Cade, or Darry?

Book Report Ideas

There are numerous ways to report on a book once you have read it. After you have finished reading *The Outsiders*, choose one method of reporting on the book that interests you. It may be a way that your teacher suggests, an idea of your own, or one of the ways that is mentioned below.

- **"See What I Read?"**
  This report is a visual one. A model of a scene from the story can be created, or a likeness of one or more of the characters from the story can be drawn or sculpted.

- **"Time Capsule"**
  This report provides people living at a "future" time with the reasons *The Outsiders* is such an outstanding book, and gives these "future" people reasons why it should be read. Make a time capsule-type of design, and neatly print or write your reasons inside the capsule. You may wish to "bury" your capsule after you have shared it with your classmates. Perhaps one day someone will find it and read *The Outsiders* because of what you wrote!

- **"Come To Life!"**
  This report is one that lends itself to a group project. A size-appropriate group prepares a scene from the story for dramatization, acts it out, and relates the significance of the scene to the entire book. Costumes and props will add to the dramatization!

- **"Into the Future"**
  This report predicts what might happen if *The Outsiders* were to continue. It may take the form of a story in narrative or dramatic form, or a visual display.

- **"A Letter to the Author"**
  In this report, you can write a letter to S.E. Hinton. Tell her what you liked about *The Outsiders*, and ask her any questions you may have about the writing of the book. You might want to give her new suggestions for a sequel! After your teacher has read it, and you have made your writing the best it can be, send it to her in care of the publishing company.

- **"Guess Who or What!"**
  This report takes the form of several games of "Twenty Questions." The reporter gives a series of clues about a character from the story in a vague to precise, general to specific order. After all clues have been given, the identity of the mystery character must be deduced. After the character has been guessed, the same reporter presents another "Twenty Questions" about an event in the story.

- **"A Character Comes To Life!"**
  Suppose one of the characters in *The Outsiders* came to life and walked into your home or classroom? Write what this character sees, hears, and feels as he or she experiences the world in which you live.

- **"Sales Talk"**
  This report serves as an advertisement to "sell" *The Outsiders* to one or more specific groups. You decide on the group to target and the sales pitch you will use. Include some kind of graphics in your presentation.

- **"Coming Attraction!"**
  The Outsiders is about to be remade into a new movie and you have been chosen to design the promotional poster. Include the title and author of the book, a listing of the main characters and the contemporary actors who will play them, a drawing of a scene from the book, and a paragraph synopsis of the story.

- **"Literary Interview"**
  This report is done in pairs. One student will pretend to be a character in the story, steeped completely in the persona of his or her character. The other student will play the role of a television or radio interviewer, trying to provide the audience with insights into the character's personality and life. It is the responsibility of the partners to create meaningful questions and appropriate responses.

- **"The Perfect Gift"**
  For this report, you will be responsible for choosing a different and appropriate gift for three of the characters from *The Outsiders*. Your gifts must be selected from the items you have available to you. Describe or draw a picture of each gift, name the person it will be given to, and explain why it is the perfect gift for him or her.

- **"Standard Form"**
  This report is a standard report in which story elements are defined and supported with examples from *The Outsiders*. Areas to include are a plot summary, character analysis, setting description, theme explanation, and a personal evaluation of the story.

Literary Terms

Complete each of the literary terms assignments described below. Students may work individually or with a partner.

PLOT

Plot is the literary term for the order of events that make up a story. Plot tells what happens.

For each chapter, write a paragraph plot summary. You may turn each summary in as you finish the chapter, or turn them all in after you have completed reading the novel.

SETTING

Setting is the literary term for the time and place a story occurs.

What is the approximate time in this century that this novel takes place? How do you know? Give specific examples. Where are the locations this story takes place?

CHARACTERIZATION

Characterization is the literary term for the development of the characters in a story into real people. Most characters central to plot and theme of a novel can be described in two ways: physically (outside description) and psychologically (inside description, personality).

Describe these characters physically and psychologically:

Ponyboy	Sodapop	Darry
Dally	Two-Bit	Johnny
Cherry	Bob	Randy

THEME

Theme is the literary term for the purpose the author has for writing the story. Three types of theme questions are: "What message is there in the book?"; "Why did the author write this book?"; and "What have you learned about life from reading this novel?"

What do you think the theme of *The Outsiders* is? Support your answer with examples from the story.

POINT OF VIEW

Point of view is the literary term for the "voice" that tells the story. A novel is usually 1st person, 3rd person (observer), or omniscient.

From what point of view is *The Outsiders* told? Who tells the story? Is the story effective when told from this point of view? Why?

Greasers and Socs Together!

For this culminating activity, you will be working together to make a bulletin board display that shows the unity that can be achieved if we try to understand people who are different than we are.

Several options are available for the bulletin board focus. Here are some ideas. Encourage your students to devise more ways to show an understanding and acceptance of others.

- Make a Venn diagram that shows the similarities and differences between the Greasers and Socs in *The Outsiders*. Here is a sample.

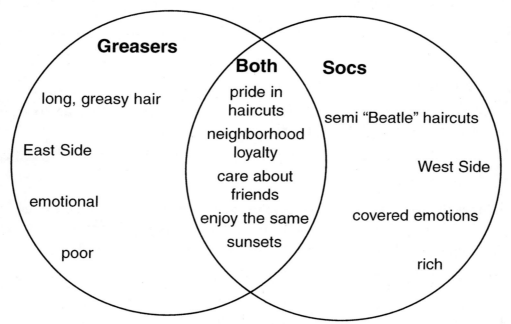

Greasers

long, greasy hair

East Side

emotional

poor

Both

pride in haircuts

neighborhood loyalty

care about friends

enjoy the same sunsets

Socs

semi "Beatle" haircuts

West Side

covered emotions

rich

- Devise a "Rules of Conduct" display that will outline exactly what both Greasers and Socs should do to live harmoniously. Here is a sample.

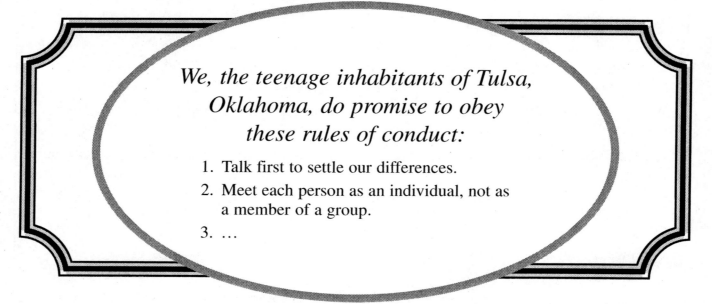

We, the teenage inhabitants of Tulsa, Oklahoma, do promise to obey these rules of conduct:

1. Talk first to settle our differences.
2. Meet each person as an individual, not as a member of a group.
3. …

Greasers and Socs Together!

Here are some more bulletin board ideas.

- Create a "graffiti" wall within the bulletin board. Supply students with marking pens and ask them to write messages from the points of view of the major characters in *The Outsiders*. Encourage messages that stress themes that are revealed in the reading of the story, such as equality, self-worth, loyalty, and open-mindedness. And, of course, all messages must be appropriate for the classroom. Here is a sample wall.

- Frame the bulletin board with paper Greasers and Socs. Each figure will be individualized by the students in the class. (See pages 40 and 41.)

- Make a bulletin board entitled "We All Share the Same Sunsets." Display the sunsets made by the students. (See page 31)

- Display poetry on a "Favorite Poems" bulletin board. (See page 23.)

- Create a "Words of Wisdom" bulletin board displaying students' advice. (See page 29.)

- Encourage students to add their own ideas to the Culminating Activity Bulletin Board.

Greasers and Socs Together!

*See suggested uses on page 39.

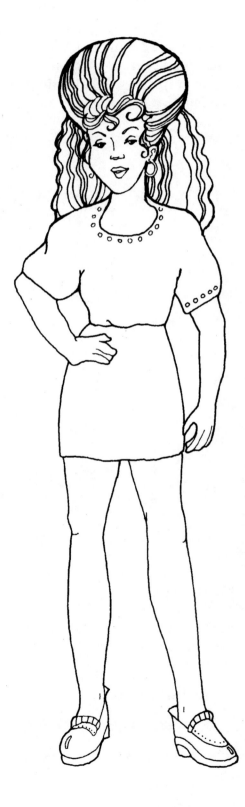

Greasers and Socs Together!

*See suggested uses on page 39.

Unit Test

Matching

Match the Greaser with his description.

1. _____ Dallas   a. wise-cracker
2. _____ Sodapop   b. tough, cold, mean
3. _____ Darry   c. frightened, abused
4. _____ Johnny   d. serious, determined
5. _____ Two-Bit   e. attractive, like a Greek god

True or False

Write true or false next to each statement below. On the back of this test paper, explain why each false answer is false.

1. _____ Ponyboy finds it easier to talk to Darry than Sodapop.
2. _____ Cherry, Marcia, Bob, Randy, Johnny, Two-Bit, and Ponyboy go to the same school.
3. _____ Greasers usually start most of the fights with the Socs.
4. _____ Darry turned down a college scholarship so the Curtis brothers would have enough money to stay together.
5. _____ Ponyboy saw Johnny stab Bob.
6. _____ Ponyboy and Johnny hide out in the church for two weeks.
7. _____ Ponyboy and Johnny think their cigarettes probably started the church fire.
8. _____ Bob's death makes Randy want to fight for revenge in the rumble.
9. _____ Dally cares about no one.
10. _____ At the court hearing, the judge realizes Ponyboy has been ill.

Short Answer

Provide a short answer for each of these questions.

1. How do Mr. and Mrs. Curtis die? _____
2. What food item do Ponyboy, Sodapop, and Darry enjoy for breakfast?_____
3. Who does Johnny idolize more than any other Greaser?
4. Why does Johnny kill Bob?
5. When Ponyboy sees Darry crying at the hospital, what does he realize about how Darry feels?

Essay

1. On the back of this paper, explain why the Socs and the Greasers fight.
2. On the back of this paper, explain the meaning of Johnny's last words, "Stay gold."

Response

Explain the meaning of these quotations from *The Outsiders*.

Chapter 3: *" 'We're always going and going and going, and never asking where. Did you ever hear of having more than you wanted? So that you couldn't want anything else and then started looking for something else to want? It seems like we're always searching for something to satisfy us, and never finding it. Maybe if we could lose our cool we could.'"*

Chapter 3: *". . . 'I gotta do something. It seems like there's gotta be someplace without greasers or Socs, with just people. Plain ordinary people.' "*

Chapter 6: *"The kid looked surprised and quit hollering. I blinked myself—Johnny wasn't behaving at all like his old self.... He wasn't scared either. That was the only time I can think of when I saw him without that defeated, suspicious look in his eyes. He looked like he was having the time of his life."*

Chapter 7: *"He kept trying to make someone say 'No' and they never did. They never did. That was what he wanted. For somebody to tell him 'No.' To have somebody lay down the law, set the limits, give him something solid to stand on. That's what we all want, really."*

Chapter 7: *" 'You can't win, even if you whip us. You'll still be where you were before—at the bottom. And we'll still be the lucky ones with all the breaks. So it doesn't do any good, the fighting and the killing. It doesn't prove a thing. We'll forget it if you win, or if you don't. Greasers will still be greasers and Socs will still be Socs.' "*

Chapter 7: *"Things were rough all over, but it was better that way. That was how you could tell the other guy was human too."*

Chapter 8: *"I figured that Southern gentlemen had nothing on Johnny Cade."*

Chapter 8: *" 'You know, the only thing that keeps Darry from bein' a Soc is us.' "*

Chapter 8: *"That's why people don't ever think to blame the Socs and are always ready to jump on us. We look hoody and they look decent. It could be just the other way around—half of the hoods I know are pretty decent guys underneath all that grease, and from what I've heard, a lot of Socs are just cold-blooded mean—but people usually go by looks."*

Chapter 9: *" 'You 'd better wise up, Pony... you get tough like me and you don't get hurt. You look out for yourself and nothin' can touch you ...' "*

Chapter 10: *"Dally raised the gun, and I thought: You blasted fool. They don't know you're only bluffing. And even as the policemen's guns spit fire into the night I knew that was what Dally wanted."*

Chapter 10: *" 'Soda, did I ask for Darry while I was sick?' "*

Chapter 12: *" 'We're all we've got left. We ought to be able to stick together against everything. If we don't have each other, we don't have anything. If you don't have anything, you end up like Dallas...that's worse than dead. Please ... don't fight anymore. ' "*

Chapter 12: *"Someone should tell their side of the story, and maybe people would understand then and wouldn't be so quick to judge a boy by the amount of hair oil he wore. It was important to me."*

Teacher Note: Choose an appropriate number of quotes for your students.

Conversations

Work in size-appropriate groups to write and perform the conversations that might have occurred in each of the following situations.

- A police officer happens to see the Socs jump Ponyboy after the movie. (6 people)

- Johnny shares his fears with Ponyboy, now that they have both been jumped. (2 people)

- Cherry decides to accept Dally's Coke at the movies instead of throwing it in his face. (2 people)

- While Ponyboy and Cherry are in the line for popcorn, several of Cherry's Soc friends ask her why she is in line with a Greaser. (4 people)

- Two-Bit and Marcia go out on a date. (2 people)

- Ponyboy, Sodapop, and Darry try to share their feelings about the tension in their house. (3 people)

- The four Socs who were with Bob when he was killed talk over his death with each other. (4 people)

- Darry, Sodapop, and Two-Bit talk about where Johnny and Ponyboy and Johnny could be, and what they should do. Dally comes, but doesn't reveal the hiding place. (4 people)

- Cherry tells Dally she will be a spy for the Greasers. (2 people)

- Johnny and Ponyboy talk about their future if they have to hide for a long time in Windrixville. (2 people)

- Jerry Wood and Mrs. O'Brian talk to newspaper reporters about the way Ponyboy, Johnny, and Dally came to the rescue. (3 or more people)

- The Curtis brothers go to Johnny's house to tell Mr. and Mrs. Cade that Johnny may be dying. (5 people)

- Dally, with the help of Two-Bit's prized possession, tells the nurses he is going to leave the hospital against their wishes. (3 people)

- Darry and Paul (the Soc that started the rumble with a blow to Darry's jaw) talk after the rumble. (2 people)

- Mr. and Mrs. Cade visit the Curtis brothers after Johnny's death. (5 people)

- After Ponyboy returns to school, Cherry, Randy, Marcia, Ponyboy, and Two-Bit meet during lunch. (5 people)

- When Ponyboy's theme is finished, he turns it in to Mr. Syme. His teacher reacts, reads it to the class, and members of the class react. (4 or more people)

- Newspaper reporters do a "follow-up" story on the Curtis brothers, six months after the night of the rumble. (5 or more people)

- Write and perform one of your own conversation ideas for the characters from *The Outsiders*.

Bibliography

Allison, Alexander, et al, compiled by. *The Norton Anthology of Poetry.* (W.W. Norton and Company, 1983)

Barrett, Norman. *Gymnastics.* (Franklin Watts, 1988)

Beatty, Patricia. *Charley Skedaddle.* (Troll, 1988)

Bontemps, Arna, editor. *American Negro Poetry.* (Hill and Wang, 1966)

Brooks, Bruce. *The Moves Make the Man.* (Harper & Row, 1984)

Busnar, Gene. *Super-Stars of Rock.* (Julian Messner, 1980)

Cole, William, selected by. *Poem Stew.* (Harper & Row, 1981)

Cormier, Robert. *The Chocolate War.* (Dell, 1974)

Daly, Jay. *Presenting S.E. Hinton.* (Dell, 1989)

Danziger, Paula. *The Cat Ate My Gymsuit.* (Dell, 1983)

Dickinson, Emily. *The Complete Poems of Emily Dickinson.* (Little, Brown & Company, 1960)

Dunning, Stephen, Edward Lueders, and Hugh Smith, compiled by. *Reflections on a Gift of Watermelon Pickle and other modern verse.* (Lothrop, Lee & Shepard, 1967)

Emrich, Duncan, compiled by. *American Folk Poetry: An Anthology.* (Little, Brown & Company, 1974)

Frost, Robert. *The Complete Poems of Robert Frost.* (Holt, Rinehart and Winston, 1951)

Frost, Robert. *In the Clearing.* (Holt, Rinehart, and Winston, 1962)

Frost, Robert. *You Come Too.* (Holt, 1967)

Hinton, S.E.: *The Outsiders.* (Dell, 1982)

Rumble Fish. (Dell,1984)

Taming the Star Runner. (Delacorte Press, 1988)

Tex. (Dell, 1983)

That Was Then, This Is Now. (Dell, 1984)

Larrick, Nancy, edited by. *On City Streets: An Anthology of Poetry.* (Evans, 1968)

Lipsyte, Robert. *The Contender.* (Harper & Row, 1987)

Mitchell, Margaret. *Gone With the Wind.* (Macmillan, 1936, 1964)

Moore, Lilian. *Go With the Poem.* (McGraw-Hill, 1979)

Polley, Maxine. *Acrobatics.* (Prentice-Hall, 1981)

Prelutsky, Jack, selected by. *The Random House Book of Poetry for Children.* (Random House, 1983)

Sandburg, Carl. *The Sandburg Treasury.* (Harcourt Brace Jovanovich, 1970)

Silverstein, Shel. *A Light in theAttic.* (Harper & Row, 1981)

Silverstein, Shel. *Where the Sidewalk Ends.* (Harper & Row, 1974)

Taylor, Mildred D. *Roll of Thunder, Hear My Cry.* (Bantam, 1984)

Viorst, Judith. *If I Were In Charge of the World and Other Worries.* (Aladdin, 1981)

Answer Key

Page 10

1. Accept appropriate responses.
2. He gets jumped by the Socs.
3. Socs pick on Greasers because they are different. Greasers fight back.
4. Their parents died in a car accident.
5. Ponyboy is smart in school, enjoys movies, drawing, and reading, and is self-conscious about being a Greaser.
6. Accept reasonable answers.
7. Accept reasonable answers.
8. Johnny, Dally, Two-Bit, and Ponyboy
9. He told her about Johnny being jumped by the Socs.
10. Accept well-stated responses.

Page 13

Explain to the students that this profile is to help them become more aware of the reality of social groups. The students may see the groups as positive and uplifting, or as negative and deflating. Encourage them to explore and share their feelings. This activity can lead to very enlightening discussions.

Page 15

1. Accept appropriate responses.
2. The Socs are too cool to show feeling. The Greasers show too much feeling.
3. Mickey Mouse was a horse Sodapop pretended was his. This horse was the only thing Sodapop ever wanted.
4. They have things in common.
5. When Cherry told Ponyboy she could fall in love with Dally, he was floored. He thought Cherry thought Dally was a hood.
6. Darry hit Ponyboy for being late. Ponyboy didn't feel loved.
7. The Socs were killing Ponyboy.
8. Accept appropriate responses.
9. a shirt, a jacket, $50, and a loaded gun
10. Accept supported responses.

Page 20

1. Accept appropriate responses.
2. Ponyboy's hair was his pride, his trademark. It made him look tuff.
3. Accept "sensitive" analysis ideas. **Note:** You may wish to provide students a copy of the poem or allow them to refer to the book.
4. Sodapop says how concerned they are about him, and how sorry Darry is about hitting him.
5. Cherry Valance
6. Johnny thinks self-defense will be proved, and he wants to get Ponyboy home to his brothers.
7. Accept appropriate responses.
8. They ran immediately to save the kids. They were not scared, just in a hurry to save them.
9. If Johnny lives, he will be crippled for life.
10. Randy wants to talk to Ponyboy about heroism and share that he is sick of all the fighting between Greaser and Soc.

Answer Key *(cont.)*

Page 25
1. Accept appropriate responses.
2. Johnny Cade was gallant, brave, and noble, just like the Southern gentlemen in *Gone With the Wind*.
3. Johnny did not want to see his mother. He had never felt loved or needed by her, so why now, when he was dying?
4. Johnny killed Bob, and Bob was special to Cherry.
5. The mood was playful, happy, etc.
6. Darry: pride   Soda: fun   Two-Bit: conformity   Steve: hatred
7. Dally came late, and when he did, Darry turned to look at him. Because Darry's eyes were on Dally, the Soc, Paul, hit Darry hard, starting the rumble.
8. They used "skin" with the exception of one "wayward" one who used a pipe.
9. Dally took Ponyboy to the hospital to see Johnny.
10. "Stay gold."

Page 30
1. Accept appropriate responses.
2. Dally couldn't accept Johnny's death because Dally really cared about him, more than anything or anyone else.
3. Now that Johnny was dead, Dally had nothing to live for.
4. Ponyboy suffered from exhaustion, shock, and a concussion.
5. *Gone With the Wind*
6. Ponyboy thought of Bob as a person he knew so little about, and he now wondered what he had been like.
7. Ponyboy insists he killed Bob.
8. Ponyboy picks up the glass and throws it away so no one will "get a flat tire."
9. Johnny wants Dally to look at a sunset, and to know that "there is still lots of good in the world."
10. *The Outsiders*

Pages 38 to 41

Create a bulletin board display of these culminating activities.

Page 42

Matching: 1) b 2) e 3) d 4) c 5) a

True or False
1. False; Ponyboy finds it easier to talk with Sodapop.
2. True
3. False; The Socs usually pick the fights.
4. True
5. False; Ponyboy was under the water at the fountain.
6. False; five days
7. True
8. False; Randy sees that fighting is purposeless.
9. False; Dally cares deeply about Johnny.
10. True

Short Answer
1. in an auto accident
2. chocolate cake
3. Dallas Winston
4. Johnny fears the Socs will kill Ponyboy.
5. He realizes Darry loves him.

Essay
1. Accept appropriate responses. The reasons might touch on the idea that Socs fight for "kicks" and to prove their superiority and the Greasers fight for pride, defense, and an as outlet for strong emotion.
2. Accept appropriate responses. Answers will touch on the idea that Johnny wants Ponyboy to stay young, fresh, nice, loving, and genuine.

Page 43

Accept all reasonable and well-supported answers.

Page 44

Perform the conversations in class. Ask students to respond to the conversations in several different ways, such as, "Are the conversations realistic?" or, "Are the words the characters say in keeping with their personalities?"

Answer Key *(cont.)*

Page 27
Use this puzzle form for the cooperative learning activity suggested on page 27. You may wish to laminate the pieces for longer use. The second time you use the puzzle pieces for grouping, tell your students they may not be in the same group as they were in before.

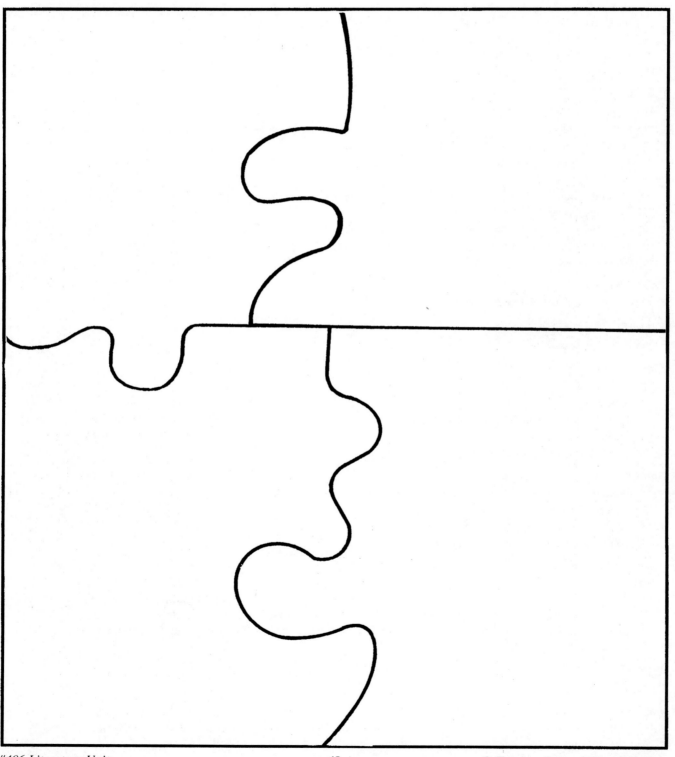